The working of Money

Ashutosh Pant

Prologue

In today's world, money is all around us. It shapes our lives in countless ways, from the goods and services we consume to the opportunities and choices we have available to us. Yet for many of us, money remains a mystery - something we take for granted without truly understanding how it works or why it matters.

This book is an attempt to demystify the world of money and economics and provide readers with the knowledge and tools they need to navigate this complex landscape with confidence. From the basics of financial literacy to the latest trends and technologies shaping the future of money, each chapter offers a comprehensive and engaging overview of key concepts and ideas.

But this book is about more than just facts and figures. It's about empowering readers to take control of their financial lives and make informed decisions about their futures. Whether you're a young person just starting to explore the world of money or an adult looking to expand your knowledge and skills, this book is designed to meet you where you are and help you take the next step on your journey.

Above all, this book is a celebration of the power and potential of money. While it's true that money can be a source of stress and anxiety, it can also be a tool for positive change and transformation. By understanding how money works and how to use it effectively, we can create a brighter, more prosperous future for ourselves and for those around us.

So whether you're reading this book as a personal quest for knowledge or as part of a formal course of study, I encourage you to approach it with an open mind and a spirit of curiosity. Together, let's explore the fascinating world of money and economics and discover all the ways it can enrich our lives and shape our futures.

Let the learning begin!

Table of Contents

Introduction to money

Before we understand anything I need
you must understand the meaning of
value. The value of a good or service
is defined by how much percent is
willing to pay for the thing and the
willingness to pay is driven by money
factors. Some factors include scarcity
of product, the utility of the product,
and the demand for the product.
When there is a limited supply of any
good and many people want I've got
the price will automatically be high
because there is too much
competition for the good.
The exchange of products or value
used to take place long ago even

before the advent of money or currency. In that time the barter system was used people used to exchange goods for other goods, and that is how people got the things they required. As you must have thought it was extremely difficult to manage and find the exact value of products and

there was lots of confusion. How could we say how much a loaf of bread is equal to one pair of shoes are how much of a pair of shoes is equals to a drum, so in that way, and in that time the value of a product were very different. There is no systematic value that all products had and that was the reason why money currency as we know it was initially created the currency in its earliest forms was in the form of sea shells, gold coins, or any other precious material that cannot be destroyed easily, and those are issued by higher authorities, usually the Kings or the churches.

Money now has acted to fill the gap as a value-given authority that specifies the exact amount anything is worth so that there is no confusion and there's no need for double coincidence to get anything. You may ask what is double coincidence? The occurrence when the wants of buyers and sellers both get fulfilled simultaneously in the process of exchange of mutually possessed goods is known as a double coincidence of wants. Both parties, the seller and buyers have to agree to sell and buy each other's commodities for a double coincidence to work.

Simply money is a medium of exchange that we use to facilitate transactions between two different people having two different wants and needs. It represents the value of goods and services that can exchange for other goods and services. That is why money has value and it can be used to purchase the things that people want to take or that people need and as it has been authorized by a higher authority it is safe and secure. Usually, the central bank of the country manages the currency of the country.

The value of money itself is determined by the several factors that determine the value of goods and services. The scarcity of money combined with the demand for it drives its value if there is too much money in circulation its value decreases because there is an oversupply of it and if there is too little money in circulation in value increases because there's more competition for the same money.

Central banks and monetary authorities of a government play a major role in controlling and managing the supply of money in circulation to ensure that the value of money remains stable over time to ensure that there is not much increase or decrease in value. They do this by controlling interest rates, adjusting the money supply, and implementing other monetary policies.

In summary, value is assigned to goods and services based on how much people are willing to pay for them. This translates into the concept of money, which is a medium of exchange that represents the value of goods and services that can be exchanged for other goods and services. The value of money itself is determined by the same factors that determine the value of goods and services - scarcity, utility, and demand.

When we talk about money, Money and wealth are often used interchangeably, but the two are not the same in any way. Money is a medium of exchange that can be used to buy goods and services while wealth is the accumulation of assets, such as property, investments, and many other valuable possessions. Money is a tool for storing and exchanging wealth, but it is not a form of wealth. For example, a person who has wealth can have many houses, and stocks in big companies, but only a small amount of money on hand. Furthermore, money can lose value over time due to inflation and change in the economy. This is similar to how when we discussed earlier, that money is also controlled by seen factors that control other goods so awesome. If there is too much money supply, it often loses value.

Money can be a convenient way to store an exchange rate, but it is not a reliable indicator of a person's overall wealth or financial well-being. Money can only be used for storing and exchanging the world, but well can exist in many other forms other than just people's money.

Types of money

From the first chapter of the book, we understood that money is an essential component of our daily. It is a medium of exchange and a store of value. Money also exists in various forms including coins, banknotes, and digital currencies. In this chapter, we will explore the types of money, their characteristics, and their uses.

Coins

Coins are the oldest form of currency that is still used to date. Although it is not very popular it is still used extensively due to the durability of coins and their ability to remain intact for years at end. While a banknote remains in circulation for around 4 years a coin remains in circulation for more than 10 years and even now we find coins from the Egyptian civilization and many other civilizations. The oldest intact coin found was 2,700 years old which was the Lydian Lion. This clearly shows how durable coins are. This durability made coins a prime way to exchange value.

Coins are small, circular pieces of metal that are typically stamped with a design or image to represent their value. Coins are typically made of precious metals such as gold, silver, and copper, or base metals such as nickel and zinc. The value of a coin is usually printed or stamped on it. Coins exist in all forms and shapes and are usually used to denote lower value such as a penny or a nickel.

Coins have several advantages. They are portable and durable, making them ideal for use in transactions. Coins are also difficult to counterfeit, which makes them a trusted and reliable form of currency. They are commonly used for small transactions, such as buying a cup of coffee or a newspaper.

Banknotes

Banknotes however not as old as coins are extremely popular. When you think about money you most probably think of a banknote. B banknote has come almost synonymous with currency and money. It is usually used to denote a higher value such as $50 or $100. Banknotes, or paper money, were first introduced in China during the 7th century. Today, banknotes are the most commonly used form of currency in the world. Banknotes are made of paper or polymer and are typically printed with a design or image that represents their value.

The use of banknotes has several advantages. They are lightweight and easy to carry, making them a convenient form of currency. Banknotes are also easy to count and store, which makes them ideal for large transactions. They are commonly used for everyday transactions, such as buying groceries or paying bills. This advantage has made it an extremely popular means of store of value. In the world of currency, it is the boss.

Digital currencies

Digital currencies are a relatively new form of currency and have not been adopted as much as the other forms of currencies. It rose due to the internet and the need for online transactions. Digital currencies or Virtual currencies are currencies that do not exist in a physically tangible form and are only stored on a computer or mobile device. They exist in the form of data on a digital ledger. There are many different types of digital currencies, including cryptocurrencies like Bitcoin, Ethereum, and Litecoin. Digital currencies have several advantages over traditional forms of currency. They are fast and easy to transfer, making them ideal for international transactions. They are also secure and transparent, which makes them difficult to counterfeit or manipulate.

The use of digital currencies is becoming more widespread. They are commonly used for online transactions, such as buying products or services on e-commerce sites. They are also used for investments and as a store of value.

Characteristics of Coins, Banknotes, and Digital Currencies

Each type of money has its unique characteristics. Coins are physical and tangible, making them easy to carry and store. They are also durable and difficult to counterfeit, which makes them a trusted and reliable form of currency.

Banknotes are also physical, but they are lighter and more convenient to carry than coins. They are typically more vulnerable to counterfeiting, which means that they require more security measures to prevent fraud.

Digital currencies are intangible and exist solely as data on a digital ledger. They are fast, secure, and transparent, but they are also vulnerable to cyber-attacks and hacking.

Uses of Coins, Banknotes, and Digital Currencies

Each type of money has its specific uses. Coins are typically used for small transactions, such as buying a cup of coffee or a newspaper. Banknotes are commonly used for everyday transactions, such as buying groceries or paying bills. They are also used for larger transactions, such as buying a car or a house.

Digital currencies are used for a wide range of transactions, from online purchases to international money transfers. They are also used as a store of value and as an investment.

There are several types of money, including coins, banknotes, and digital currencies. Each type of currency is different in its way. Coins are physical and durable, making them ideal for small transactions. Banknotes are lightweight and convenient, making them ideal for everyday transactions, as well as larger transactions. Digital currencies are fast, secure, and transparent, making them ideal for online transactions and international money transfers. Each type of currency has its unique characteristics and uses. The uniqueness of each type of currency makes them unique and useful in their way.

History of money

Money is a ubiquitous and essential component of modern society, but its origins and evolution are often overlooked or misunderstood. The history of money can be traced back to the earliest human societies. Continuing from lesson one, the origins of money can be traced back to the earliest human societies where trade and barter were the main primary means of exchange. Far before money was invented people traded goods and services directly for one another exchanging one item for another based on the relative value. For example, a hunter might trade a deer for a basket of fruit or a potter might exchange pottery for a bag of rice. However, over time trade

become more complex as societies grew bigger and became more and more interconnected.

It became even harder to facilitate trades directly and a need for an intermediary agent for the trade of value was required. This requirement was tried to be filled by many things and commodities that were standardized these were the first forms of currency. Some of these standardized units included cowrie shells, beads, or precious metals like gold and silver. Even basic goods like vanilla were used as currency. These early forms of currency made it easier to buy and sell goods and services since they could be easily recognized and traded for other goods. As trade could be done easily due to these standardized agents, they were even extensively developed to make the trade even easier.

The earliest form of currency existed in the form of a cowrie shell which is extensively used as a form of currency in China as far back as 1200 BCE. The shells were small, durable, and rare, which made them an excellent form of currency. Around the same time in other parts of the world, precious metals like golden silver were used as currency since they were easily recognized and had an intrinsic value. Huge quantities of gold and silver were transferred through the silk road specially to be converted into coins and other forms of currency.

The Greeks are often attributed to the development of coins as a form of currency. The Greeks began minting coins from around 600 BCE. That is called the start of the coin, which is still in use. Now coins were made of precious metals like gold, silver, and bronze, and were stamped for the image of the ruler or a deity to guarantee the value. Coins quickly became popular as a form of currency, since they were very portable durable, and extremely easy to recognize. Due to this coins can easily be said to be the oldest form of currency, having been used for almost 2600 years.

In China, the Song Dynasty (960-1279 CE) was the first to introduce the use of paper money as a form of currency. Paper money was first used in the form of "jiaozi" or "exchange certificates" that were backed by the value of the goods they represented. Later, the Chinese government began printing paper money that was not backed by any physical commodity but was instead guaranteed by the government's ability to collect taxes. This slowly developed and was transported via the silk road to many different parts of the world. Although the knowledge regarding paper currency already existed long ago they were only mass adopted by the 17th-18th century.

In the middle ages, the most basic forms of banking and credit began to emerge as an important component of monetary systems which laid the foundation for the current monetary system which is a complex system of lending and borrowing. Merchants and traders began to develop complex systems of credit and debt, allowing them to conduct business without the need for physical currency. This system of credit and debt would eventually lead to the development of modern banking and finance, which are essential components of the global economy today.

Up to a century before all currencies were pegged to gold meaning all currencies could be exchanged for a fixed amount of gold. This made the currencies very secure and safe. All currencies being pegged to gold meant all currencies could often be exchanged at near the same exchange rates. But currencies were slowly shifted from the gold standard to a floating system where the exchange rates of currencies were directly affected but the economic health of the country the currency was associated with.

Or simply, Today, most countries use a system of fiat currency, where the value of the currency is not tied to any physical commodity but is instead determined by supply and demand in the marketplace. This system allows governments to print money to meet the needs of their economy, and it allows for greater flexibility in monetary policy.

The modern monetary system is based on the use of central banks, which are responsible for managing a country's money supply and ensuring the stability of its currency. Central banks use a variety of tools, such as setting interest rates and buying and selling government bonds, to control the money supply and maintain price stability.

The modern monetary system also includes the use of electronic money, such as credit cards and digital currencies like Bitcoin. These forms of currency are becoming increasingly popular, as they offer greater convenience and flexibility than traditional forms of currency.

The history of money is a fascinating tale that spans centuries and thousands of years of human civilizations. From the barter system to the new emerging cryptocurrencies the monetary system and the definition of currency have changed in many forms but have remained the same as a value-giving body. From the earliest days of trade and barter to the modern monetary system, money has played a central role in human society, facilitating trade, commerce, and economic growth. While the forms and uses of money have changed over time, its importance as a means of exchange and store of value remains as strong as ever.

Digital money

Continuing from where we left from the second lesson, digital currency or also commonly known as cryptocurrency, is a form of currency that exists totally in digital form and is stored in. A ledger as a data entry. Unlike the other conventional currencies, they are not regulated by any government or any other governing body. They are created by a process known as mining and are maintained through a decentralized network of computers.

The most common and well-known of the cryptocurrencies is Bitcoin, which was created I n2009 by a person or a group of people by the pseudonym Santoshi Nakamoto. Since the inception of this first cryptocurrency thousands upon thousands of cryptocurrencies have been created are being created in a daily basis. Each cryptocurrency is unique in its way differing from each other based on features and capabilities.

The primary and important feature and advantage of cryptocurrency is its decentralized nature. Rather than being controlled by a central authority like a government or bank they are maintained by a network of computers around the world who store a copy of the ledger which makes hacking and mistakes nearly impossible. This also makes it resistant to censorship or government interference, as well as being more secure and safe at the same time.

Another advantage that digital currency has over conventional currency is its low transaction fees. Unlike traditional payment methods like credit cards, which charge merchants a percentage of each transaction, digital currencies often have very low fees or no fees at all. This can make them a more cost-effective option for merchants and consumers alike.

Digital currencies are also being mass adopted with countries like El Salvador even declaring it as a legal tender allowing its citizens to use it for all purposes as if it was any other conventional currency like the dollar.

But like everything digital currency is not also only roses and silver, it also has some unique problems and challenges. Because they are not

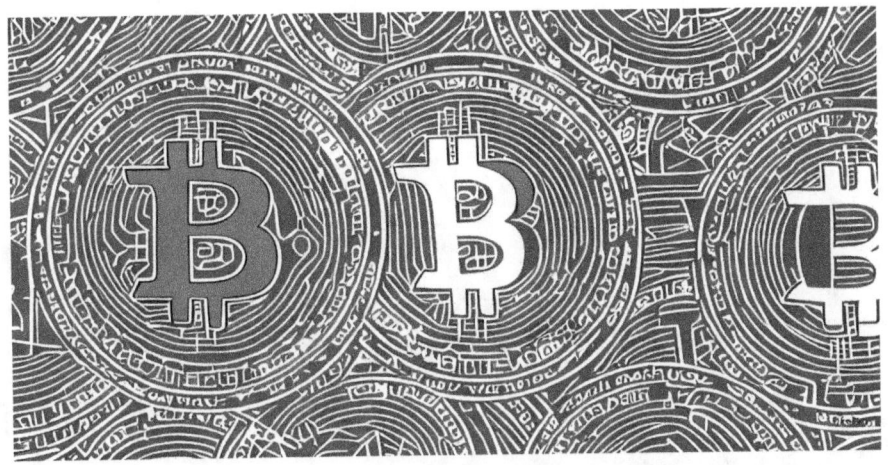

backed by a government or central authority, their value can be highly volatile and subject to rapid fluctuations. In addition, they have been associated with illicit activities such as money laundering and the financing of terrorism.

Despite these challenges, digital currencies have gained significant popularity in recent years, with many investors seeing them as a potentially lucrative investment opportunity. As the technology behind digital currencies continues to evolve, they will likely continue to play an increasingly important role in the global economy.

Central Banks

Central banks play a major role in the economy of a country and the region under its influence. The decisions of the central bank have a major share in the significant impacts on businesses, governments, and individuals.

Central banks are financial institutions that play a critical role in any economy. They are responsible for regulating the money supply, controlling inflation, maintaining financial stability, and promoting economic growth. Central banks are often associated with monetary policy, which refers to the actions they take to control the supply and cost of money in the economy.

Although they may have varying degrees of independence, central banks are always owned and operated by governments. In some counties, central banks are not heavily regulated by the central government of the country as in other countries, and the central banks operate with a high degree of autonomy, while in others, they are subject to heavy government, influence and control.

What are the main functions of the central bank? It regulates the supply of money in the economy. They do this by controlling interest rates which affect the costs of borrowing money for businesses and individuals. When the interest rates are lower, borrowing is cheaper and people are more likely to spend and invest which can stimulate the economic sector positively. But when the interest rates are high, borrowing is more expensive, which discourages spending and investment, which will reduce borrowing and economic growth will slow down. Central banks also play a critical role in curbing or controlling inflation. (Inflation refers to the average increase over time in the rate of average price for goods or services). You must have noticed that the price of the goods does not stay the same over time and you slowly increase, this phenomenon is known as inflation. If the inflation is too high. It can erode the value of money leading to a decrease in the purchasing power of the individual and leading to economic instability. Central banks use various tools to control inflation, such as addressing the interest rate and regulating the money supply.

In addition to regulating the money supply and controlling inflation, central banks also have a huge responsibility to maintain financial stability. This means ensuring that the banking system is safe and sound and that the banks have enough capital to observe losses and withstand economic shocks. Central banks play a huge role in responding to financial crises by providing liquidity and support to the banking system whenever necessary. This is why the central bank is also known as the Bank of Banks.

Central banks are also responsible for promoting economic growth. They do this by using monetary policy to stimulate investment and consumption, which can increase economic activity and create jobs. Central banks may also work with the government to implement fiscal policies such as tax cuts and infrastructure spending to promote economic growth.

Central banks are financial institutions that play a critical role in the economy. They are responsible for regulating the money supply, controlling inflation, and maintaining financial stability. The central bank has various tools and policies to achieve these goals, including interest rate adjustment, open market operations, and regulatory oversight of the banking system and economy as a whole. Central banks operate with varying degrees of independence, and a subject to political and economic pressures, which can impact their effectiveness.

Monetary Policy

Monetary policy is an extremely powerful tool that governments can use to manage economies. It is issued. By the central bank. It involves using various instruments to control the supply of money and interest rates to achieve specific economic goals that the government wants to achieve. It can be called the most important policy to control the economics of a country.

The history of monetary policy can be traced back to the early days of banking and finance. For centuries the government and banks started manipulating money in various ways to either fund wars or other expensive projects. However, it wasn't until the beginning of the 20th century that modern monetary policy and its functioning took place.

One of the major developments in the history of monetary policy for the creation of the federal reserve system in the United States of America in 1913 AD. The Federal Reserve was established to serve as a lender of last resort to banks during times of financial crisis, and it was given the authority to regulate the money supply to promote economic stability. Since then monetary policy was and has been a critical tool for governments around the globe to control and better manage their economy. Today, central banks in almost every country use various monetary policy instruments to control the money supply and achieve economic goals.

The Objectives of Monetary Policy

Monetary policy of a country can have different goals and motives based on the country, the economic situation of the country, and the goals of the country. Some common goals of a monetary policy include maintaining price stability, creating/increasing employment, and facilitating better economic growth. Maintaining low and stable inflation rates is one of the primary goals of monetary policy as a whole country. High levels of inflation can have huge negative effects on the currency of a country often eroding the value of the currency, which

makes it very difficult for individuals and businesses to plan and invest.

Tools of Monetary Policy

Central banks use different tools to manage and implement monetary policy. Some commonly used tools include:

1. Open market operations: The most common tool of monetary policy is open market operations. This involves the buying and selling of government securities, such as bonds, to control the money supply and influence interest rates.

2. Reserve requirements: Central banks can also influence the money supply by setting reserve requirements for banks. This refers to the amount of money that banks must hold in reserve against their deposits.

3. Discount rate: The discount rate is the interest rate that banks pay to borrow money from the central bank. By raising or lowering the discount rate, central banks can

influence the cost of borrowing and lending.

4. Forward guidance: Another tool of monetary policy is forward guidance, which involves guiding markets and investors about the future direction of monetary policy. This can help to shape expectations and influence market behavior.

Problems with monetary policy
Like anything in the world monetary policy also has its problems and criticisms. The most common problem and criticism of monetary policy is its inability to achieve the desired economic goals by itself. For example, if the economy is facing structural problems, such as high levels of debt or low productivity, monetary policy may not be sufficient to promote growth or job creation.

Also, Monetary policies around the world are criticized over the time it takes to bring a tangible result. It can take months or even years for changes in interest rates or the money supply to have a noticeable impact on the economy, which can make it difficult for central banks to respond quickly to changing economic conditions. Some critics argue that monetary policy can be unpredictable and destabilizing. Sudden changes in interest rates or the money supply can lead to volatility in financial markets, which can have negative consequences for businesses and individuals alike.

Monetary policy is a critical tool that governments use to manage their economies. By controlling the money supply and interest rates, central banks can influence economic activity and promote stability, growth, and full employment. However, monetary policy is not without its challenges and criticisms. It can be difficult to achieve desired economic goals through monetary policy alone, and sudden changes can lead to unpredictability and instability. Nevertheless, the importance of monetary policy cannot be overstated, and it will continue to play a central role in the management of economies around the world.

Fiscal Policy

Fiscal policy alongside monetary policy is used by the government of any country to manage its economy. It is basic government spending and budgeting. It refers to the use of government spending and taxation to influence economic activity.

Governments use fiscal policy to influence the level of economic activity of a country. During times of economic downturns government may use fiscal policy to stimulate demand and create economic growth while conversely, in the time of inflation or overheating of the market. The government may use fiscal policy to reduce demand and cool the economy.

Any fiscal policy is made of two major components government spending and taxation and the government can use both of these to influence economic activity. For example, when there are times of economic downturn score, make me increase spending on infrastructure projects, volume roads, and bridges to create jobs and stimulate demand while in the time of inflation or overheating increase taxes to reduce demand, and slow the economic growth as a whole.

One of the major components of fiscal policy is the multiplier effect. This effect claims that government spending can have a far larger impact than the initial investment by the government itself. We can understand this through an example in which if the government spends $1 billion on developing the infrastructure of a city through infrastructure projects, it may have an impact on the economy of the city of greater than $1 billion as the workers employed in the project will spend their wage in the city, other surrounding supporting structures will be created by private investors to make the maximum gain from the government spending, etc. The multiplier effect can help to amplify the impact of fiscal policy interventions.

However, there are numerous limitations that a fiscal policy needs to tackle. One of the main limitations is that it can be difficult to time fiscal policy interventions correctly. For example, if the government increases spending during a recession, it may take some time for the spending to filter through to the wider economy and stimulate demand. Conversely, if

the government reduces spending during a period of economic growth, this may lead to a reduction in demand and a slowdown in economic activity. Timing is therefore critical when it comes to fiscal policy interventions.

Another major limitation of the Fiscal policy is that it can be very difficult to implement. Governments may hesitate to increase taxes or reduce spending even when it is required because it is very unpopular amongst the voters. It makes governments hesitant to implement these changes as it could reduce their popularity and reduce their chances of winning the election in the end.

In addition to all the limitations, fiscal policies can also have various unintended effects and consequences. For example, increasing government spending can lead to inflation if the economy is already operating at full capacity. Additionally, tax cuts may not always lead to increased consumer spending and may instead be saved or used to pay off debt. Therefore, it is important for governments to carefully analyze the impact of their fiscal policy interventions on the economy.

Despite all these limitations, fiscal policy remains an important tool for governments to manage their economies. During times when the economy of a country is down fiscal policy interventions help to stimulate demand and increase economic growth. Conversely, during times of inflation or overheating, fiscal policy interventions can help to reduce demand and slow economic growth. Fiscal policy remains an essential tool for governments to manage their economies and promote economic growth and stability.

Future of Money

Money is a field that is witnessing some rapid developments in recent days. Money is changing rapidly with emerging technologies and trends reshaping the way we think and process the world of finance.
A major trend we can see in recent days is of cryptocurrencies such as Bitcoin and Ether. These currencies as explained in previous chapters can function without a central system of central banks. These digital currencies rely on complex algorithms to ensure the security and integrity of transactions. While cryptocurrencies have faced some regulatory challenges and concerns over their environmental impact, many see them

as a promising alternative to traditional forms of currency.

Another trend that has extreme prevention and has the possibility of shaping the future of money is digital payment systems such as mobile payments and e-wallets. With the rise of smartphones and other mobile devices, more and more people have already started using such platforms to do the daily transaction and maintain their finances. These platforms make it extremely convenient and easy to manage your finances. The trend is especially pronounced in developing countries where people lack basic facilities and access to traditional banking services which makes these banking options, extremely convenient and easy.

Blockchain technology is also playing an increasingly important role in the world of finance. Essentially, blockchain is a decentralized ledger system that can be used to secure store, and verify transactions. This technology has the potential to revolutionize many aspects of financial trading, supply chain management, and more.

One was the most exciting possibilities could be using blockchain technologies for decentralized finance (DeFi) platforms. These platforms allow the user to access financial services and products without the need for intermediate trees such as banks or brokerages. While DeFi is in its early stages many see it as a really promising alternative to traditional finance.

The future of money also raises an important question about financial literacy and responsibility. As digital finance becomes more popular its relevance increases exponentially and people know and learn how to manage finances effectively. People need to be educated on how how to protect themselves against fraud and other forms of financial crime.

Ultimately, the future of money is still being written. It's impossible to exactly predict what to look like. However, one thing is clear emerging technologies and France are fundamentally Rishab in the world of financial economics. The current technological revolution is similar to when the first money in the form of seashells was created or when we had the first paper money printed or when the first coin was minted, and this revolution is happening right in front of us. So let us enjoy this revolution and keep on exploring.

www.ingramcontent.com/pod-product-compliance
Lightning Source LLC
Chambersburg PA
CBHW070828220526
45466CB00002B/785